LYFE

POETRY

LYFE

BY

ANTHONY ORTIZ

-DEDICATED TO THE ONES WHO HELP YOU GROW-

CONTENTS

DREAMS   1

WHITE CHRISTMAS   3

WHAT WE WON'T BE   5

VIOLETS   7

HAVE A DRINK   9

NEW YEAR   11

TROPHY WIFE   13

PRENUP   15

SLOW LANE   17

INSTANT BADDY   19

SHOTS   21

MY OWN WAY   23

LAWD HAVE MERCY   25

ELECTION 2020   27

SIDE KICK   29

VALENTINE   31

BLINK   33

GOLD DIGGER   35

NEW SHOES   37

FACE IT   39

AZTEC   41

THICKER THAN WATER   43

RAMEN   45

BLUE WHITE RED   47

FIRE   49

THE PLUG   51

SOPRANOS   53

WALLS   55

5 SENSES   57

TATTOOS   59

RIDE OR DIE   61

MIND FULL   63

SUMMER LOVE   65

NO TIME   67

SPLIT   69

PAY DUES   71

LIKE THAT   73

ICE   75

HOMELESS   77

SINGLES   79

GLADIATOR   81

DM   83

COMBAT   85

DREAMS

I had a dream.

That we all receive the success we need.

That we fight for love and peace

And love is reached,

Daily.

Commitment reaching past your 80's.

I had a dream...

That one day we will rise.

Above the clouds and beyond your eyes.

See the hope and read the signs

But we decide our future.

We define the new ones

Cuz we inside the unit.

Small thoughts

Keep us all lost

And it's all fog till we found.

When we all walk

It's a small walk

So let's knock till it's our town.

WHITE CHRISTMAS

Presents aren't present.

I wrap myself up cuz it's colder where I'm heading.

Either show them that you love em or indebted.

Where the time go? When you counting every second.

It's a White Christmas.

Known for the high grade.

I got the city coming at me like a mind state.

But I'm too new for these moves, and these eye shapes.

I'm just holding tight, ride it till the vine breaks.

It's a White Christmas.

Gotta reach a quota.

Ima put it on the line, you can blow it.

I don't do it for the time or the moment.

I got God on my shoulder till my family getting rich...

It's a White Christmas.

WHAT WE WON'T BE

She just walks by, walk by, walk by.

They just want guys to know they lonely.

As they walk by, walk by, walk by.

Framing those eyes in gold but lowkey

Hiding those lies, those lies, those lies.

Taking your time, each step moves slowly.

Watch it go by, go by, all night.

She gone hold tight to what we won't be.

VIOLETS

Roses are red so I bought you some violets.

Beauty's a word, but I see you define it.

Feeling the pressure, we turn that to diamonds

Cuz lions be climbing this jungle and island...

Exotic.

I've never been so about it.

You've never been iconic.

Hands on your body and timing.

We go around and the rounds are combing.

I Love it

Cheers to the subject.

HAVE A DRINK

From the rooftop, Love is overrated.

Everybody loves till you seeing complication.

Take another heart, they know the operation.

Yeah, there's plenty of fish.

But why just give up?

You ain't seeing the potential like you never been up.

You ain't talking, but they calling and you never pick up.

You just don't want to admit that you ever hiccup.

Have a drink.

NEW YEAR

Where the time go?

2018 like an eye soar and I'm more reserved.

Government finally legalized the earth.

Fake news make you take it to the turf.

DT tryna bring about the purge and we lost.

"Don't Shoot", what we screaming to the cops.

No rules, when they showing you the law.

Don't move, be a statue or they draw.

Red and Blue

Gang members in the House and Senate too.

Yeah, they can't faze that a New Year bringing change.

We heard it before, you started carrying your weight.

They got carried away.

And we still carry the state.

TROPHY WIFE

I see you.

But you ain't living how you talking.

Take it all for granted, it's sad you never clocked in.

Find yourself a boss when you looking for some objects.

He looking at the options and you looking for a prospect but,

Where the Love at?

How much to get the love back?

How many times you show me that a come up had a come back.

Right?

That's a Kodak Life.

Snapshots and redoes.

You tryna get that fixed

And they dying just to be you.

PRENUP

She with me in diamonds.

See me, design it. It's a perfect fit.

Luxury riding.

Hit the Bahamas with our perfect kids.

Living the Dream.

Visit the Keys and then we right back.

I'm on a call

She at the mall doing 5 laps.

5 bags, she can barely hold it.

We just riding the wave

Next door to Billie ocean.

I found me a Queen.

Bought me the Kings and got iced out.

Future looking bright like a lighthouse.

Then Lights Out.

I never saw it coming.

Never signed a prenup.

I never set a budget.

She be making 7 figures.

And she never doing nothing.

Fixing on retiring

A Victim of these judges.

SLOW LANE

How can you not drive a speed?

Wishing you just lost your keys.

You going 20 under.

I got places to be.

And this lanes for me.

You making us suffer.

It's easy, just turn right.

Believe me, that's your life.

And everyone else

Can push limits and pedals as well.

I'm ready to pass you.

Start a trend that's past you.

But I can't move till it's free.

Horn blast can't move in my seat.

Let's go!!

INSTANT BADDY

Champaigne and bubbly

My selfies are daily

To show you I love me.

Cuz life is a beach

And I cater to no one.

I fly in cuisines

Aces on deck and I fly in my queens.

We just the bosses that write what you read.

Caption a dream.

SHOTS

Sweat dropping from my forehead, got the chills.

Grab the mic, get the go ahead to rock a lil.

Every step I'm getting closer to the battlefield.

Feeling like a Guru taking Mass Appeal.

There ain't no greater feeling.

They going crazy

And they play me till we break the ceiling.

Break it down, make it loud and I make you feel it.

Make a million, make a difference and I make a killing.

In 40 minutes 40 seconds

Couple thousand listen.

About our mission

Took a shot and I ain't ever miss it.

MY OWN WAY

With no mistake

Break the box, smash the photo frame.

I'm from the flame,

Life is hell and I got more to raise.

Drinking on that gas to fuel the motorcade.

It ain't enough.

I'm giving up just when the motor break.

I'm finding solace in the silence.

I know that our past will bind us.

Behind us they wanna pray.

But I don't mourn that way.

We born with less

But we blessed to take another step.

Tryna stay afloat but I don't know the depth.

I had to go my own way.

LAWD HAVE MERCY

You picture perfect.

Hope the picture worth it.

Pitch a curve with every curve

And help her fix the curtains.

I can make it rain

And we can keep it current.

On some one-night stand biz

That keeps occurring.

Love is war but she keeps her courage.

Quite assertive when she keeps it flirting.

Give me purpose while I preach a sermon.

Lawd have Mercy yeah you put your work in.

Tryna be the one and only version in the worship.

ELECTION 2020

I need to pick a side.

We don't need to know your mind.

Just who to fight.

Tell me more about economy

Then food we buy.

Making money off our backs

But this do or die.

That's right.

We control the vote.

Let em know, we ain't feeling this.

We ain't bout to go and build your pyrimids.

Tell me something new.

Not the news, this is serious!

They just sound the same.

This a game

Across periods.

SIDE KICK

I can see you.

Beauty, they wanna be you.

Show them just how to walk.

No talking about redo.

We.

Come together that's art.

Go the distance no car.

And show them bitches you are.

And that's it.

A new star.

The past 6

Couldn't charm with magic.

Then we met.

And you the reason we kept.

Moving and raising the temp.

It's only fair that you left

For the right one.

Shine, call you diamond.

I see your real worth.

Dime to the nylons.

VALENTINE

We weren't lost but

I feel like I found you.

In a world with so many to crowd you

Your beautiful.

Every glance I hold a memory past.

Presently our future carry's me to love.

No sentence can fully explain.

The way the face, body and taste.

Can make my heart race.

But I will never run.

We will walk together.

BLINK

When I look at you, I reminisce.

Blue skies, back and forth the carriage went.

Like tide turning the ocean in Maryland.

I never dare to blink.

I see past you

Of a past you.

Those mountains cry but outlast views.

Daggers out those eyes like she had to.

She never dares to Blink.

GOLD DIGGER

Why you know the name

While you look through every counter?

Retail, addicted to chains and the power.

Girl you look up through the shade from the tower.

Red bottoms, S&M whip by the hour.

I know.

I know.

The devil wears Prada.

Down to burn it all cuz

They done know the cost of.

I know.

I know.

The Devil loves drama.

You know that love is fake

When you take it to the Oscars.

NEW SHOES

You are the irreplaceable style choice.

The only relationship I'm ok with strings attached.

Help a deaf man define his voice.

But our pairs never seem to match.

Its vibrant

I can feel the soul.

Always there to lift me up

When I'm feeling low.

How can I walk without you?

You the last pair I believe in

After the others I outgrew.

FACE IT

I had to step away.

Movie star life like

How long could this take?

Along for the fate

But I long for the days

That are lost in the page.

Give it all, Get me paid.

I never wanna take, I'm only tryna give.

Paying the cost right? I even left a tip.

Leaving you broke when I was only tryna fix.

Leaving the coast and I been back since.

But I be following my drive.

Caller #9 I be calling for the prize.

Falling from the dive

Got me calling on my pride.

Now I'm following the tide.

And got my flow straight.

Collecting cash

From the past and the old ways.

When we get together, I see mosiac.

We the diamonds in the ruff but we more jaded

Get together till we old faces, Face it.

AZTEC

Scrapping the pavement, igniting the block.

You tucking your chain and hiding your watch.

Smoked in the street or die in Iraq.

Fighting for future we die for those knots.

Stockings were empty, now buying them stocks.

He one in a million, I'd die for a shot.

And one in a million would die for a watch.

I roll with the ridas too high and get lost.

Taking our shot with collapsible stocks.

You gunna get burned like you passing the La.

You study my shit, you passing the bar.

Damn, I'm a beast

Don't step to me dog you just mad at the meek.

Leaving them marked when I'm handling beef.

Preparing for war but I pray with the piece.

Collecting my ends and I pray for them weeks.

Look at these pups keep their ass on a leash.

Invincible flow that's Immortal Technique.

THICKER THAN WATER

You were taken.

But never taken from our thoughts.

Up the river, stomach pains, a few knots.

Life's a struggle

Several fights, a few lost.

Hold you down when you get out.

Is what we grew off.

You were too young and raised by the system.

Transfer to maximum, creating the distance.

But you always stayed true never playing the victim.

With every letter I grew through your wisdom I risen.

To a man with a vision.

Pen, pad and some rhythm.

Issued rifle, scope and precision.

Young disciple your story is written.

Hards times we thought of you and its strength that was given.

Theres no embrace at arm's length.

Always by my side, keep reaching till arms ache.

Made a reservation it's ok we gone wait.

Till your number up.

Yeah, that's something to celebrate.

RAMEN

I put my life on the line.

My life in these rhymes.

Connecting the dots, I bring site to the blind.

I need a cut so Imma bring a knife to the grind.

I was hungry before I had a license to drive.

He stare in the mirror and see life in his eyes.

Decide to grab a pen like a mic and outline his life.

Let them hooks fly like shells his mind ignites.

Tryna make a dollar for his daughter.

So he slaughters beats like a beast.

So she can go and be a doctor.

Rhymes got a lil buzz, Orange juice Vodka.

Working on the rush like I'm running through sponsors.

Paying all my bills like I'm born to eat ramen.

Like, "that dude got beef, let's go feed off it."

BLUE WHITE RED

Now I done took a different path.

I enlisted to get lifted and run the track.

We play for keeps, slow squeeze

And hope you make it back.

Yeah, this has to be selfless.

Train till your sides burn like Elvis.

Yeah, we fight for the flag.

And we fight for the chance.

To make another man fight for they land.

Take one step and fight with they hands.

We just tryna make friends while they fight in the sand.

So lace up, face front.

And know that pay cuts keep you angry enough

To show them what you made of.

Not everyone made tough.

Enlist.

FIRE

Keep that a hundred

We back the gunner

Drum filled with numbers, It's deep.

Weed pack a hundred

We stash a one up

Rollin up a quarter a piece.

You like the fire I need.

I light you right by the tree.

We keep it hot in degrees.

I know your spot by the beach.

There never been so many Ops

But we on top of the key.

THE PLUG

Starting off the day.

Call it wake and bake.

I don't even play.

Smoke Amazing Grace.

Lifted it off the face.

See me count my cake.

Call me honor roll.

On me on the low.

OG in the bag.

Flip it a-la-mode.

You ain't see me pass.

Feed me, see the grass.

I just show up

4 the money in the bag.

SOPRANOS

Family First.

Capo got men for dirt

But plan it first.

And we feel the perks.

This chess I played back in Rec.

I made connects that made the rest.

Then laid to rest.

10k no longer pay the rent.

We got the cops to make the moves

And place the steps.

Untouchable.

I bring the union 2 the block

Till the function through.

But I'm never in the state

Or accustom to the noise.

If It wasn't for the Feds

You'd never hear my voice.

WALLS

I'm inside my head

It's an 8 by 10.

Writing on the walls

Beating on the pans.

I can see em all

Leaning by the fence.

I can see the guards

Feeding by the gram.

Lights!

Take to me to the days I get 2 fight.

Take me to the gate with me and mine.

I just got the word after they open.

Use it for the roll I need a light.

Waiting for my number is it time?

100 on my books - I'm eating nice.

I ain't even do it in the first place.

Give me back what's left and make it right!

5 SENSES

I wanna See how you dream.

You a dream when you see me.

You and me

Leave it all behind us out in Kings Street.

You a queen bee.

You hold me down

Hold the crown.

Only hear them when they

Moving pounds, moving loud.

Now and later we just move around

We allowed.

Missing how you smell like every flower in town.

You my type.

Touching every key you keep in site.

And you the ride.

We gone take together give me time.

I'll rearrange it.

Show me how you like it

You just biting while I taste it.

Imma give your senses 5 reasons 4 its patience.

TATTOOS

Skin deep.

You can read.

There's some ink in my story.

I got a piece.

Rest in peace.

They ain't picking this for me.

I got a dream.

Writing "King"

That's the theme of my quarter.

Around a sleeve

Take a knee.

Getting demons in order.

RIDE OR DIE

Rearview see the lights.

I ain't tryna die tonight but I know I'm the type.

Grip tite on the wheel.

Happy meal to the backseat.

Need to pull it over, See a corner.

Can't trap me.

I can see your gun & your vibe moving close.

But I aint tryna move until you tell me I can go.

Show you what you need.

No, I didn't leave a scene.

Kept my hands on wheel.

Why you reaching for your piece?

I ain't living like you see.

And you wonder why we beef.

Know I ride it how I live.

Tell my daughter I'm a King.

MIND FULL

Time never stops.

And life's just a pause.

We think we the boss

But we living till we drop.

There's peace in the lack of time.

Give me back those years

I didn't live for the moment.

Own it.

SUMMER LOVE

She lost her heart to the summer love.

Falling out the sky like an angel does.

Think she found the Queen bee, major buzz.

At her destination but it ain't enough.

Get her voice herd like she gaining trust.

Diving headfirst like she dangerous.

Arm sleeved up; in the pain she trusts.

Singing love songs with her alias.

Feeling on her chest like a patriot.

Tell me life a party, Tryna cater it.

Shouldn't bet on us cuz I'll pay for it.

NO TIME

What do you say?

To a new place.

Pack a suitcase.

Get some room service while we roommates.

We gone pick it out.

Out the crowd like a bouquet.

Never play it safe

It's a race to the crusade.

Moves made were full frame.

Butane like Luke Cain.

Explore the night, we arrive like Bruce Wayne.

Another dark night

No fights and loose change.

Just tryna live it right.

No time for new plays.

SPLIT

I'm hurt, no fuck it, I'm angry.

We've been going at it for weeks

But it doesn't seem to daze me.

Don't blame me, just stop.

Don't play me, this lost.

You trying to find what you already dropped.

Go ahead, reminisce, those memories.

You tryna light a fire from old chemistry.

This the end to the friends like enemies.

Let's not pretend some things not meant to be.

PAY DUES

Ain't safe when the doors locked.

No time for the Porshe when you don't stop.

No stops when you got you a whole block.

That's stock and you can't let it go by.

That's fine but she can't buy your whole time.

That's why they did life and I own mine.

I'm right by my doggs in the moonlight.

We sign when its time.

Down for the ride

Down for the life.

Tell them take two.

You can go that way, or you make do.

You can make stacks, let the money make you.

Just a few bags.

Go and pay dues.

LIKE THAT

Heaven hard to reach.

Live below the law

Every corner street.

Pushing every border call

Take my time to eat.

Break it down and blow it off.

See the finer things.

Why she gotta show it off?

Borderline a freak.

ICE

I'm a little ahead.
Call it ahead of the wave.
Head in the clouds
Heaven around
I head for the bank.
Taking a dime
Taking her out
She taking the raise.
Taking her time
Making her mine
Then making her pay.
This is the price
This is night
This is the game.
This is the light
Reflecting the ice
You hold by the flame.

HOMELESS

Wish I had a place to rest my head.

Concrete on my feet, back, head, two legs.

Few beg when we down.

But they still walk around me

Cuz they don't see the crown

When they found me.

They just wanna throw it back.

Not even clean enough to go to mass.

They only see me when they photograph.

Like we can really make it right from your pity.

Make sure you bring a camera

When your giving in your city.

Got my hands out but no one tryna feel me.

I'm a dreamer too!

I had it all & didn't mean to lose.

I still see heaven on the scenic route.

One day I'll see you there.

Already got family that I'm meeting there.

Life is suffocating all I need is air.

I needa hear a prayer.

Hands together, We...

Can find an answer to all the ashes

We burnt up on the streets.

SINGLES

84' Pontiac, 05'

Red and Blue illuminating low light.

Lightheaded we ride like Coal mines.

Born sinner my only co-pilot.

Head down while you focused, no blinders.

From the street to the web with no spider.

If they feeling you late that's all fibers.

And I'm alright with

No-one really knowing your man.

I can vent from a distance.

Knowing the fans will feel this.

She feel tips more

Then she feel stripped.

Its a lonely road to those Millions.

Make the money known and watch chameleons

Appear friends.

Make waves till the Peir ends.

Never drowning me though cuz I count on lows.

Every 1 matters so I count em slow.

GLADIATOR

Blood ties, I'm tied to Rome.

I'm tired of fighting, realizing I might be throne.

I might be known.

I'm leaving despite the code.

I'd die for Rome.

Got a wife at home and a sword and shield.

Take my land they absorb the steel.

When they done you can mourn the field.

Keep marching we got more to kill.

It's an uphill battle but it's more than hills.

So, we Push.

About done with campaigns.

Loosing mad names for mad days, the gods late.

Got faith and got played, behind cages we grow now.

This the legion.

Pledge your allegiance.

Fight with a purpose

Grab sand from your region.

We live to die free but

We'd die for our freedom.

DM

What's this? A new feed from old news.

Same story, new problems, no clues.

I drop singles.

I don't make these old moves.

Time takes out queens we go through.

Play chess.

Don't check on old tunes.

Playing back the same track, the shows through.

COMBAT

I be walking 10 clicks and I ain't seen a soul.

Start thinking to myself, what am I fighting for?

I light a cig, look at my homie to the left.

He took a step... and took his last breath.

There ain't nothing left.

We in shambles so we scramble, take the last scent.

Revenge is past tense.

We gather, master a plan of terrorist disaster.

Set off to find the man who makes children a bastard.

We got simple weapons.

But in our hands, this is village wreckage

With some pillage second.

Arrive our eyes are red and beat.

We push, because we warriors don't care to sleep.

We careless creep into the village, now where is he?

Bring em forward or I'll find em... I guarantee.

They glare and see the flare in me

And point in the direction I can barely see.

We move.

Silent and deadly

Blood shot and we heavy.

We never blood shy

Got the runtime so we ready.

Reach the door, knock twice, there's no answer.

Shotgun blow back the door backwards.

Pop Pop, drop boxes and more canons.

Everyone hit, team six got more damage.

Took 2 to the chest with no bandage.

I got 3 men down, and no package.

Just looking in our eyes we all manage

To see they made

Students into soldiers while off campus.

www.ingramcontent.com/pod-product-compliance
Lightning Source LLC
Chambersburg PA
CBHW07005710426
42740CB00013B/2855